"THROUGH MY EYES ALL ABOUT ME"

Dedication
"A Mother to Me"

During the time that I was in my foster home with Vera is when Roberta, my godmother stepped into my life and she really showed me much love. She did not have any daughters so she took Vera's two grand daughters and me as her god kids. At first I did not like her because she was so into God and all she would say is "just trust God". She still says that to this day. But over the years she helped me a lot I never dreamed that I would have someone stand by me even if she did not agree with some of my choices. Roberta told me stay close to God. When I chose to be in bad relationships or thought I was going to lose my mind she would talk me back into my right mind. God -mother was the one that gave me the front money that helped me open my salon. I can say that because of her my kids and I never went hungry and we never had to worry if the lights would get cut off. She just was a mom to me and I want to dedicate this book to her. Thank you, god mom for loving and nurturing me; and to all the other moms that stepped in when I needed guidance and thank you mom for having me.

INTRODUCTION

1979 appears to be my best recollection when I was young girl. I remember being this curious little six-year old black girl, born to Cindy who is Portuguese. I really don't think she was very proud to bring home this black child. I had two brothers, aged four and five. My mother did not expect her first child to come out dark skinned; she thought I would come out more of a lighter shade, like high yellow. Unfortunately, I came out a little darker than what she had expected. My hair was not straight, it was a little more curly toward course. I believed this was a real disappointment for my mother. My brothers Aaron and Carlos looked the same. They had the same color skin and the same kind of hair, but it was a lot different for the boys being dark skinned than her daughter to be dark. From that point on I thought my mother and I really never connected. I didn't understand. Why did she act so indifferent? Could my skin color really have effected her this way?

Years later, another sister came. Crystal, beautiful long flowing curly hair, a real pretty light skinned baby girl. I don't really remember her walking and talking as a baby, but she was the one who spent time with grandpa and grandma. Everyone finally got the light skinned baby they wanted. Crystal was the golden child, so she stayed with the grandparents a lot. Crystal reaped all the benefits. My mother continued to have children. Along came Pepe Jr., Tamika, Charmain and Gregory. These last four children had all the Portuguese features. Just like my mother, they all had the fair skin and good hair. My mother has had eight children in all.

While living with my mother and two brothers: Aaron and Carlos, I remember a time when were young. We were playing around being happy and mother worked at the hospital. At the time, I thought it was the greatest time of my life. My mom was "legally" employed and married to Alphonse, who is the father of Carlos. As a child, I can remember being very mischievous. An example of this would be when we were sitting around the table. Mother had cooked dinner, she came in and we had all cut the front of our hair. I was the ring- leader. Aaron and I had gotten spanked. Mom could not believe we had cut the front of our hair to where you could see a bald spot. But my other brother, Carlos was really smart. He patched his hair back into his head so mom did not notice his bald spot. Mother did not give him a spanking. After all the spankings were handed out, Carlos reached down to get his spaghetti with his fork and his hair fell into his food. We all started laughing and laughing. That was probably the best time that I could remember us having good times.

Chapter 1: Through My Eyes All About Me

It all began when my Mother started having problems with us and decided to leave her husband Alphonse. Stability for us was over, and then mom finds out she's pregnant again. Mom begins hanging out in the clubs trying to find herself. She runs across a man named Larry, but everyone calls him Pepe. He seems to be this wonderful man. Promises her he's going to take her away from all of her problems. Pepe says he going to make her rich. He wines and dines her, persuading his way in. My mother is so impressed with him that she brings him to meet all of us. Pepe's family owns a farm. All I remember about the farm is the chickens, cows and horses. I also remember the great dinner we had and all the running around on the farm we did. I finally think, WOW, this is going to be so good! Mom has finally met a nice man that is going to stick around. We're actually going to live well and Pepe was going to be the father that we all wanted. Unfortunately, this is not how it turned out. Pepe was in the military for awhile, then he came back to Sacramento to live with his parents. What mother didn't know was that Pepe was this big time pimp, he had got into this pimping game when he came back from the military. Pepe did all of these nice things to make my mother believe that the things she will be doing will be benefiting all of us. My mother started slowly doing prostitution. I was six years old, getting ready to turn seven and mother decided to move to New York City. Mother is out prostituting, pick pocketing the unsuspecting New Yorkers. Being that I am the oldest, I am the designated babysitter. I had to watch my three younger siblings, and for a seven-year-old that is really difficult and hectic. Mother could not handle all of us so she decided to send us back to Sacramento. For my mother, living life as a prostitute in the big apple was far more important than raising her children. So off to California we go to live with Carlos' grandmother Mrs. B.

For approximately a year or two, she was very good to us. She clothed, sheltered and fed us. While going to school things were going swell. We were happy. Mother was not financially contributing to help us. Grandma B. was taking care of us alone. We were getting hot meals and our personal needs were being met. We were very happy living there because she did the things that a parent was supposed to do. Our baby sister, Crystal, didn't live with us because she got to live with are grandparents. Mother continued to come in and out of our lives for a couple of years. When she would grace us with her appearance, she would come in a limousine and take us to the biggest mall in Sacramento. To show that she cared, she would let us shop and change our old clothes in the store. We would walk out with new clothes on. Afterwards, she would always take us to McDonalds. My grandmother had two other grandchildren living with us named Delisha and Rodney. They would come along to, and ride in the limousine and get new clothes and McDonalds. Mother could not leave them out. Mom spent about an hour or two with us, then she would take off in a car or go catch a plane to wherever she lived. We would not see her for one, two or maybe even six months. It depended on when she felt like it or if she saw it fit to come back to see her children.

Mother started coming back from time to time, I believe because she did not have any money, and she wanted to get a welfare check to survive on. So, mother pulled us away from grandma's house. This time grandma went to court to get custody. Grandma could only get custody of her real grandson, Carlos. Aaron and I were not her real grandchildren. Grandma tried to get custody of Aaron and I, but the courts gave her a hard time, so we could not stay with grandma. Once again we got uprooted and had to leave, never to return to grandma's house as kids.

Mother takes us and crystal, we move from city to city. Her prostitution is getting stronger and stronger, were growing up getting older, mother is pregnant with little Pepe. We are not quite sure if Pepe is really Big Pepe's. Mother never got a DNA test. Pepe could be the son of another man named Kenny. Kenny is another pimp who she was prostituting for. Pepe and Kenny where the two major pimps that mother was with, but Pepe was her main pimp for the long haul.

By this time I'm around nine years old, Aaron is eight and Crystal 's a couple of years younger. My baby brother Pepe's arrival is just around the corner. Mom is still prostituting while pregnant. Pepe Jr. is finally born and he becomes attached to me just like he is my son. He probably feels this way because I was the one practically raising him. I taught him how to talk and walk and I made sure he was properly cared for. When Pepe Jr. cried I wiped his tears away. At this point we were on the road. We traveled through Texas, Florida, and New York. We went through Atlanta, moving from place to place. Mother is out prostituting and she's pregnant again. Time passes and mom has my sister Tamika. She claims this man in Massachusetts is Tamika's father. We have been so many places over the years. Mom decides to leave Pepe. But as usual he makes multiple returns and each time, mother takes him back. When is the madness going to end?

Healing Words

Lost because of color don't allow no one to dictate your life by the color of your skin. Love who god intended you to be he gave you your color on purpose.

Chapter 2:My MOM'S. Is Off the HOOK

From 1981 to 1983 we are stuck. We didn't know what to do. After all, we're all very young. My mom has had six children. Her only means of supporting us was prostitution. Abuse to her was a normal, it was an every day thing. I'm acting as if I am the mother of six children, and all I know is prostitution and abuse.

I remember one time mother took me with her on the hoe stroll while Pepe was with the other kids. I stayed in the car while mother went prostituting in New York. I stayed in the back of the car, from time to time mom would come and check on me. While she was working the streets in New York City, I had to go with her and still to this day cannot understand why. Maybe it was for protection, or maybe she didn't want to be out there by herself. She would bring the guys to the car and do her thing. Mom would get a motel room to do her thing and I would be in another room. Afterwards, we would go back out to the streets.

My mother did things a mother should not do to expose a child to the things. She thought nothing was wrong with what she was doing because she traveled and got to bring her kids with her, but she was destroying us. If there were any kind of values or morals to be learned it was foreign to us. All we knew was prostitution, pimping and hoeing. I don't think that's a positive thing to have your children involved in.

I remember another time when we were out in Las Vegas. My mother did not come back to the room. It was check out time, we had no money so the people ended up putting us outside. We sat there with our suitcase for hours and hours. We had one pack of stale doughnuts, I believe the kind that comes six in a pack. I would split up the doughnuts trying to feed the kids. Keep in mind these are not my kids. They are my brothers and sisters. I feel like I'm their mother. This was a very difficult time. We felt like we where being abandoned. We kept thinking, "what's going to happen to us?" Mother has us out here in the middle of nowhere. At first, we have no clue where we are. Then, I find out we're in Las Vegas. We don't know anyone here. Mother has us stranded in no man's land, and she is no were to be found. Finally, after three hours, they come to get us. They bring no food to eat. We leave this location and then mom and Pepe goes to another hotel. They pay for our room. I breathe a sigh of relief! Then the same night, mom goes out and makes probably twenty or thirty thousand dollars. She comes back and gives me some money and tells me to put it up, and tells me not to let Pepe find out about it. She says that we will be leaving him, she just needed to stash away money. just like clock work, Pepe comes and mom gives him money. They fill up two queen size beds full of money, jewelry, and rings, it was one of those Mike Tyson or Evader Hayfield fights. I'm not sure which one it was. Mom got this man for a bunch of money. Maybe two or three days after that happened, mom and Pepe are nowhere to be found. I get a call from mom she says pack up all the stuff cause she is going to keep Pepe away. So I have everything packed and the cab comes and gets us, mom gets away, and we finally leave Pepe.

We are headed for Massachusetts, but on the way the car mom is driving spends out of control from the ice on the road. The car almost goes off the freeway mom tells us to get on the ground and pray and the car stops right at the over bank. There was no harm done to any one of us or the car, mom gets out and makes sure everything is okay, it is we get back on the road.

Eventually we get to Massachusetts and mom gets this little cottage with an upstairs and downstairs overlooking the water, snowing and very beautiful. We can play. We have things we can do, we're a family again, but we barely have any kind of education. We really haven't been going to school that much so mom says she is going to register us in school.

Well with all her good planning and her intentions, Pepe is back on the scene. Once again, our needs go by the wayside. After Pepe's arrival we eventually move again. This time it's Texas . Mom and big Pepe get a house in Texas and they actually register us in school. We all are happy thinking we'll be for a long while. As usual this happiness doesn't last very long. Going to school for us became less and less. Trouble would always loom around us when we were not doing things kids should do, like going to school and having school- aged friends.

For instance, my little brother Pepe Jr. managed to get the keys to Pepe Sr.'s car running it into the neighbor's house doing some major damage. Now we can't stay in this area because they don't have money to pay for the damages done to that women's house. So we pack up everything and we are off again. At this point we're driving through all these southern states. Mom is continuing supporting us by selling herself. Pepe in the meantime is beginning to really physically abuse mom. They keep going through the same stuff over and over again. Pepe beats her up one day then mom says she will leave him. This vicious cycle goes on and on. Finally, mom gets fed up and we are in Sacramento, CA again were mom is dropping us off again this time with someone we don't even know. My mother's new friend Angela said she knows this lady that she leave her kids with all the time so it would be good for us to go their until they come back from there hole stroll adventures.

Healing Words

Prostitution is a choice not an inheritance.

Chapter 3: Does anyone love us

Its 1984 and mom leaves us with a lady we called granny. She was very neglectful towards us. Granny did not feed us properly and we were not bathed. This was a very bad environment for us. I can recall that when we did get food, there were roaches in the food and crawling all over. Another example of her neglect was my brother Pepe had a piece of glass in his foot for almost a month. Granny never attempted to get the glass out. It wasn't as if it was a small piece either. It was a very large piece of glass. I tried to get it out but was unable to. His foot became swollen and infected. I thought the doctor's were probably going to have to amputate it. The glass eventually came out when my aunt came to visit and took him to the hospital Pepe Jr. was very lucky.

Things where so bad where we were that my brother Aaron would go out on the streets begging for money, so his sisters and brothers could have food to eat. Finally, Jillhad came back to check on us. She was appalled about the condition we were living in. We get relief. Aunt Jill takes us in. Aunt Jill has a friend who ends up helping her. She and Aunt Jill split us up. Aunt Jill takes three of us and her friend takes the other three children. But this situation doesn't last very long. My grandparents tell Aunt Jill that she should not be taking in three children. You see Aunt Jill has recently gotten married and she already had two children of her own. My grandparents went on to say how these kids are Cindy's and she shouldn't worry herself behind it. Then my grandparents spoke the unspeakable. They said you need to put these kids in a foster care or in a receiving home. Aunt Jill tried to speak up for us. She told them that she could do this if she had some assistance. She asked them to take Crystal and that she would keep me and Tamika and her brother John could take Aaron and Pepe. Aunt Jill was trying to make sure that we stayed with family but my grandparents were saying no, let them go to the children's receiving home. They said this was nobody's responsibility but Cindy's.

At this point my mother was in prison. She robbed or stabbed someone so she was going to do time. Auntie goes on what her parents said, so we go to the children's receiving home. Aaron and Pepe go into a foster care home to live with a minister. Tamika and Crystal and I go into foster care home together. We end up living with this foster lady for two or three years. It's now 1986 and mother gets out of prison and she decides she wants her kids back. She is going to do everything the system tells her to do. She begins counseling sessions. So far she is getting to all her appointments and does everything she is suppose to do.

During this healing time mother gets pregnant with Charmain who is born in 1987. Mom is not sure if Pepe or a man named Kenny is Charmain's father, so she names her after herself. The closer it gets for mom to go back to court to get us back mom cannot seem to stay away from Pepe. She is court ordered to stay away from Pepe. Since mom complied with all the court orders and did her training, we end up going back to live with mom. She is in a two-bedroom apartment off of Rio Linda Blvd. But as usual mom doesn't stick to the rules. We are not even back a week and she's on the phone with Pepe. Mom is making plans to run away with us to be with Pepe. Mom is making plans to be back in the same life style that got us taken away in the first place.

At this point I'm in the seventh grade. Tamika and Charmain are on the scene so there are more kids to take care of if mom goes with Pepe. I was the babysitter and mother to my siblings. I was so hurt inside knowing that mom was planning on going back to this man who had her on the streets and beating her. When mom went to prison Pepe disappeared, never came around us never concerned about the children and now she's going to go back to him. Like we were not important but he was more important to her. As time goes by, I contemplated calling the social workers so they can come and get us.

My brothers and sister's really wanted to stay with mother so I kept quite; it got really bad, because mother did get back with Pepe and he's very abusive I saw my mother get beat down to the point where you couldn't even see her face. Pepe would beat mom with a shoe, iron and throw her through tables. He would beat her with anything he got his hands on. He would beat her down if she would look at or say anything to his pimp friends. If mom passes by without saying excuse me she would get beat down. Mom didn't know what she was suppose to be saying, but she never stayed away from Pepe for a long period of time

Healing words

Abandoned by love punished by pain but some how knowing that I rest in god's hands.

Chapter 4: Someone loves me

We end up going back to Las Vegas in 1987 and live in a mobile park with Pepe. Mom continues to say she's going to leave Pepe, but I see that it's never going to happen. Mom is out working on the streets again. Mom's not paying attention to us at this point because she has become a drug addict. Mom and Pepe snort so much cocaine hour after hour. They are always high and drinking. They couldn't provide the proper living for us, but they made sure they had the most expensive Cognac and their supply of cocaine. We're just living out here doing things kids should not be doing, but this is the only thing we knew.

While living in Las Vegas I met this sixteen- year old boy named Trent. He shows a lot of interest in me. So I say to myself, oh well he's nice and cute. Maybe he might be able to take me away from all these things that are happening to me and all the bad things that are going on in my life. He started coming around and started playing basketball with my brother Aaron. He asked him what my name was and Aaron told him and gave him my phone number. We started talkingevery day.

While Pepe is out getting high all night and my mom is out working the streets I find other things to occupy my time. Trent comes over and sits on the porch with me and we talk, talk and talk and he can't believe that a 14 year old could be going through all these bad things and being a mother to all these kids. Trent tells me that he just wants to take my brothers and sisters and I away from all of this and come live with him. But I'm only 14 and he's 16 so there's no way he can take all of us with him.

Trent was living with his big sister and she had just had a baby and could not take us in. Trent was feeling so bad, we would sit out on the porch and he cried with me. We would stare out at the stars until four in the morning. I'm feeling sad, but the next day he comes back and I'm thinking that I have never felt or experienced love like this before. I know that I'm young but now I feel that someone loves me. Trent listened to everything I said and he helped me with the kids while my mom was going out to work on the streets. Trent never asks me for sex or any of the bad things I see every day.

Five months pass by and Trent said to me, Angie I want to take all of you with me but I can't. I'm very afraid. If you continue to stay something will happen to you because your mom never comes home and when she does, she is not bringing any money or food. You also said that PePe is going off. What if he puts you on the streets? So Trent asked me to runaway with him and I say yes. I packed up my stuff and that night PePe comes home and I sneak off and meet Trent up the street and we go to his house. That next day my little brother Aaron must have told my secret. Aaron must have thought that he would have to be the parent so he tells PePe where I am. PePe comes to Trent 's house and knocks on the door and Trent opens the door. PePe is at the door and asks Trent where is she. Trent response was that he didn't know where I was and that he had not seen me. PePe says you know where she is. She's in your house and you better send her out before I call the police on you. Trent responded if you don't get away from my door I'm going to call the police on you for making Angie's mom prostitute herself and leaving her all alone with all those kids. I'm in the bathroom listening to what going on and I can't believe that someone really care about me to stand up to PePe and protect me. Trent then tells PePe to get off his steps now or he would push him off. PePe ended up leaving from Trent 's house. I tried to call my worker and tell them where the kid's were but it was too late. PePe and my mom packed up the kid's and left Las Vegas .

I end up staying with Trent for about two months and our relationship has changed to an intimate one. We began having sex. This should have never happened but it did. I really believed he loved me but I was a child and should have been loved by my mom not a boy. Trent 's sister ends up telling me I have to go because she has too many people at the house and she had just had a new baby. She could not take on any more responsibilities she ask me is there anywhere else I can go. I told her that I was a foster kid In California and I guess I can go there. I really did not want to. I didn't want to leave someone who finally loved me for me. But I had to go so I called my worker and they sent me to a receiving home for about two days and then she sent me a bus ticket back to California.

I finally arrive back in California. Thank god my foster mother that I stayed with in the beginning takes me back into her home. At this point I'm in the eighth grade going into the ninth life as I new it would never be the same. I'm

no longer a virgin so I'm
experienced now. I've had sex. It's a whole new thing now. My foster mom
discovers that I'm not a virgin and she takes me to the clinic to get me put on
birth control. I try to do the right thing but my mindset has changed. I'm not
a little girl anymore. I don't want to
do the things that I did when I was a kid. Church was fun then but now I
don't want to go to church everyday of the week and truly I don't want to
obey the rules. I want to do what I've been doing. I am now rebelling. I am
wondering why folks are trying to put rules and regulation on me. I can't take
it any more. I want to move from here. They are trying to control every part
of my life. Grandma Virginia didn't want me to talk to Trent anymore
because it was long distance and she didn't want me to run up her phone bill.

   I end up calling my social worker Cheryl and she moves me and I can't
believe what I did. Now I'm really in a fix. I go to this new foster home where
they don't even buy food. She's on a diet. I guess I have to starve because she's
on a diet. The foster mom only bought me four bras the whole time I was
there. This stay didn't last very long. I get moved to another foster home. It
doesn't get any better. The foster home I moved to have a child molester in
the midst. I hurry up and called to be moved. My social worker moved me to
the children's receiving home. I end up just a runaway from the receiving
home with this girl named Tina. I felt that no one should have to deal with
this. If I stayed gone long enough my social worker would find me a good
home this time. While I was on the run I met some people and lied to them
and told them we where from Chicago . We end up staying with this guy
name Chucky we did not even know him but he does not harm us at all.
Chucky doesn't even ask us for sex. This is when you can say God's got your
back. The next day we returned to the receiving home. About two days later a
lady named Vera comes to take me to her home to live. I go and she becomes
my foster mother. For the first time in my life, I have a real mom. I end up
staying with Vera for a long time.

Chapter 4: part 2/someone love's me

It's 1988. I'm going in to the ninth grade. I'm a cheerleader for Grant High School. I am finally moving on with my life. I meet this boy named Otis. We get to know one another. We end up sleeping together. We were just starting something and my mom calls. My "real" mom tells me she needs me. I tell her I'm not going back into that life. I told her that I'm in a good home now and I'm not going to leave. But mom just keeps calling me. It's around summer time so I start feeling bad because my little brothers and sisters needs me so I ask a good friend Gilda to run away with me and she says yes. We wait until mom sends us money, then we get on the plane and go to Washington, D.C.

Not to long after we're in D.C my mom is giving Gilda a bad time saying that Gilda wants her man so now Gilda wants to go home. So she calls her old boyfriend Lawrence my best friend and he sends for Gilda. And she goes back home to Sacramento I stay and take care of my sisters and brothers. Charmain is a baby and my mom is pregnant with my brother Gregory. I'm not feeling very well and these kids are irritating me. I don't want to be here. My mom is with Gregory's dad and he is a pimp. He is beating her all the time. She is still working the streets pregnant.

My mom takes us to meet one of her friends Lela who is a Madame. She runs a home full of working girls and owns a bar. We stay there for about a week and my mom come back to take us. I don't want to go. My mom is mad but I don't care so I stay. Lela has three successful kids from what I think is successful should be. Her son John who is a big time dope dealer has lots of cars and about three or five houses. Lela has a daughter Lisa that's in college and Nikki getting ready to go to college. My mom comes over from time to time for me to watch the kids so I still see them. Lela ends up taking good care of me.

I'm not feeling good so Lela takes me to the doctors and I'm pregnant! I can't believe it .I'm only 15 years old. What am I going to do with a baby? We go back to Lela's house and she says she want me to stay and go to school. Get a good education she tells me. She also says that she wants me to get out the game so I won't have to deal with maybe becoming a prostitute like my mother. Lela then says that she is willing to stick by me and help me but I would have to have an abortion. I could not see to do that. This is my baby. This is a part of me. Some one I can love and be a good mother to. I can be different than my mother. I call my social worker and tell her to send for me.

Once again I'm in D.C the social does send me a ticket and I'm on the bus back to Sacramento. When I get there I tell her where my sisters and brothers are and I think I'm going back to Vera house but they didn't get hold of her in time. So I end up at this other foster home with Reada and she makes an appointment for me at the clinic and said you need to have an abortion. I'm six months pregnant. She expects me to have an abortion and I'm feeling my baby kick. Reada says you probably don't even know who the baby's father is and he probably doesn't even remember you. I didn't care what nobody says. I called my foster sister Michelle and tell her to come get me and give me a ride to Del Paso Heights. That is where I hung out at and that's were I went to school. She comes and take me right to where Otis is. He looks down at my stomach and says what's wrong with you and I say I'm pregnant and it your baby. Otis then says I have not seen you in six months. I say it's your baby so he says ok. Otis does the math and to him it's right. But I was really telling the truth. I had only been with Trent and Otis. My foster mom Virginia had put me on birth control pills and a year had passed by before I had met Otis. Otis gave me his number and told me to call him the next day. So I do and we talk and I told him this foster lady wants me to have an abortion and Otis says don't have abortion I already have one son and I will help you with the baby. I believe him so I have my son but before the baby comes Vera let me come back to her home.

Now I'm back in school doing well getting A's and B's doing well. I'm on the right track. It's time for the baby to come and Otis comes to me and tells me he has to do some time in jail. He had gotten into some trouble. He said that he would have to do two months and that he would not be there for the birth of our baby. I'm disappointed but there's nothing I can do. The two months past and Otis get out and bring his friend over and they look at my little boy Otis Jr. and Otis Sr. says he looks just like me. He proudly claims that this is his son Otis Jr. This is my pride and joy. My first baby boy and I love him to death. We spoil him rotten.

Otis and I were not really together and tried to keeping what we had going but we were so young and both filling are self and it was hard to be to gather. Otis stated sleeping with one of my best friend and my cousin and that messed me up so I decided to secretly date is friend and that really did not play out good because he was really heart when he found out and we never had the same conation agene I did love Otis but we were to much in to being the hottest things in town and we just new it was best that we just remand friends. I decided to try to live my life the best that I could .

Vera had a lot off responsibility so I would just try to make it easy for her she already has two of her own grand kids Amber and Kea They are younger than me and now Vera has me and my new baby but we have a tight family. Amber and Kea are just like sisters to me. They treat little Otis just like he's their family. Life is good. Then my little brother Aaron calls and says I can't take it anymore. Mom's got us all over the place. Mom had us in Hawaii, Florida, and Texas. Mother was hoeing in all these different states. We keep talking and he is watching the kids while she out working the streets and I don't know what to do. So I ask Aaron to tell me the location he's in and he does. I contact the social worker and they find them. But my brother Gregory and sister Charmaine can't come. They are not in the foster care system in California. They were never foster kids in Sacramento so they have to stay in DC. Little PePe, Tamika Aaron and Crystal get sent back to California. I get to meet them at the airport and they are dirty and filthy. They are so nasty; they look as if they have not taken a bath in a very long time. Tamika started telling us that a man molested her and he had put his thing in her mouth and says I don't want any hot dogs. Crystal starts crying. She does not say much but I can tell something happing to her. Crystal never tells me but I just know, Aaron never says he was molested but he tells me that Charmain and Gregory were still in that home. After hearing all of that I let the kids know that they get to go back to there old foster homes. I get home and I call child protective services in DC and tell them were Charmain and Gregory are but they get there too late. My mom had already come and got them. About a year later I called down to check up on Gregory and Charmain and found out that my mom was in prison again. I'm thinking what am I suppose to do? What's going to happen to Gregory and Charmain? They really don't know my mom. Gregory was born in jail and is only a year old and Charmain is two and now they're in protective custody. So I'm worried about them being with someone that will hurt them. I'm just worried and fell like they need me and I can't help them but I have a son and need to think about him so I just try to put all this stuff out of my mind and take care of me and my son.

Healing Words

Holding on to finding my first love.

Chapter 5: Not this time

I'm in the 10th grade and doing very good in school. I meet this guy at school name Anthony and we start dating. I really like him and he likes my son. That makes it much better so now were boyfriend and girlfriend. We end up having sex and I get pregnant. We are so young and I already have a baby that is only one year old. I'm not ready at all so I talk with Anthony and we decided that it would be better if I had an abortion. I also sat down with my foster mom Vera and told her that I was pregnant and that I was going to have an abortion. Then Vera told me that she doesn't believe in abortions, and Vear told me that if I had a abortion that would have to leave. So I had the abortion and I had to leave Vera's foster home. Anthony and I decide that this relationship is moving too fasts and we could not handle it so we break up and just remain friends. I end up moving into another foster home with this lady name Kim. She was more like a sister she was about three years older then me so I though this was so cool. Now I can do what I wanted but because I had a son and he was very important to me I just could not get all the way out there and I put him first. What every my son needed, I was able to get for him. I was employed at McClellan AFB. I purchased my very first car. Life was finally good to me.

Healing Words

No understanding of life, so easy to take a life, be a responsible person not a careless one.

Chapter 6: that's my Daddy

I decide at the end of 1990 that I wanted to find my dad but I had no idea how to go about finding him. My mom had given me his name along time ago and that's all I had to go on. So one day I told Kim what if I called 411 and she said try it, but it probably want work. So I called and some white woman answered the phone. I said I'm looking for a man name Leo and she said her husbands' name was Leo. I replied I'm looking for a black man she then said my husbands is black but he's not home. The woman continued by asking me how could she help me. I introduced myself to her and told her the reason for my phone call. I was looking for my dad. I also went on telling her the name that my mother has given to me was Leo. Angela then said that her husband had been looking for is long lost daughter name Angie. So now I'm stunned because she knows my name. She then tells me that he will be home in about two hours and she will have him call me. He does and he knows all my family and asks me could he come and see me I told him ok and I have a son and we would be happy to meet you.

My dad informed me that we had already met. He then he told me that my mom stopped coming around after I had turned five. So he actually knows me but I didn't remember him so we make plans to meet that following weekend. It's finally time for me to meet my dad. I hear a knock on the door. When I open the door he looks like my twin. We're identical. My dad takes me to his house and he has a girl there. He tells me that this is my sister Dewanna and we look a like. We talk and get to know one another. We have a good time and promise to stay in touch with one another. But that does not happen. The next time that I see my father or sister isn't until I turn 27 years old. My father got on drugs and just feel off the face of the earth. I was so involve led with my life I just don't try to fiend him.

Years passed by and I happen to run into one of my aunts and she had just talked to my sister Dewanna. I called Dewanna and she tells me that daddy is getting married, and stating going to church and is a Christian know and I was so please to hear this so I decided to call him. My father tells me he's in the Bay Area. Daddy asked me if I would like to come to his wedding, I say yes, so I go and I had a good time I met is wife and I just real liked her. She asks me if she could be a mom to me and I though that this was so nice of her and I told her that that would be nice. Patty my dads wife had to boy twines and we all fit just like a family but something happen and my daddy just stop calling me and stop coming to see me and his wife did not even try to keep in touch I called all the time but nothing so I just stopped trying it did heart me bad because I just wonted my daddy to be proud of me like I was so proud of him for over coming drugs and finding some one to love him. I hop one day he will be proud of me and love me like he loves my sister Dewana,.

Healing Words

Daddy where were you? I needed you to help me build my character.

Chapter 7: Living on my own

The year is 1991 and I'm ready to move out on my own. Every thing is ok. I just want to be on my own. I am 17years old. I'm ready to get emancipated so I ask my worker and he tells me no I'm too young and not ready. I don't listen to him and I do what it takes to get emancipated. I kept my job to save money and get me an apartment, go to the judge and get my emancipation. Now I'm working taking care of my son loving on him and every body loves him. He is so smart. Seems like he's reading the books, but he's just memorizing them. Otis is getting so much love.

I finally have my own apartment a one bedroom, finally my own place, where I can call home for me and my son Otis. I'm surviving and making it. Yes I'm working and taking care of my son, and we are very happy.

I met this girl named Susan who lived upstairs from me. She's a cool girl who lives with her father. We start hanging out and we became friends Susan's father treated me like one of his kids. He watched over Otis and me, he made sure I had the things I needed. He also made sure that no one hurt my son and I. My neighbor Susan introduces me to this guy named Michael. He seems cool and nice so we began talking to each other. At this time I'm just turning eighteen so I think I'm grown, cute slim and my hair is long, I have it going on. So I can talk to whoever I want to. This guy comes over one day while my brother Aaron is over visiting. Aaron takes my son Otis to the park for a little while. We talk and talk and he seems really cool. Out of nowhere he starts getting a little .aggressive with me. He's like let's kiss and I say I'm not feeling you like that. He still tries to kiss and touch me. Now he starts coming on to strong. All of a sudden he begins to over power me. I'm telling him no! I don't want to have sex with you! He then he pins me down and begin to rape me. I'm devastated and yelling telling him to get off of me, he doesn't he just continues to rape me. Finally he gets up then he leaves. I called the police soon after he leaves and they come and take a report. My upstairs neighbor father comes home and asks me what's going on, what happened here. I tell him what happened and he could not believe it. He knows this guy. He is a friend of his. He tells me this guy is thirty-seven years

old and is sorry that his daughter introduced me to him. Then he leaves and I believe he went to the club at McClellan AFB. He's looking for his friend. He can't believe this guy put himself in this situation. He is going to kill his friend if he finds him but he doesn't find him. He is disappointed that he would put his hands on me. My neighbor continues chasing after him. No luck. Thank God. For some reason I have this strange relationship with Big Pepe. He's still like my father even though he did us kids really, really bad. He comes by my house and I tell Pepe what happened to me. Now Pepe is out looking for this guy to hurt him real bad for raping me. Now the police is looking for him, my neighbor's father is out looking to hurt this man and now Big Pepe is out looking to hurt this man who raped me. The guy is now running for his life. I'm just devastated that bad things keep happening to me. Eventually they the police find the man who raped me and come to find out he had raped another girl the day before he raped me. It was the same situation. They where introduced and he acted like he acted with me all nice. Then he waited for a long time before he raped her. He ended up getting ten years in the pen and he was wanted for murder in another state. I just thank God that I was able to get out of that situation in a healthy state; I didn't die or get even crazier in my head, even though it took me awhile to recover from the rape. I didn't let the rape affect me like it would someone else in that situation, maybe because of the life style I was used to seeing. Unlike many rape victims, I was unaffected. I just buried the rape just like all the other
stuff that I had went through. I just continued to bury it in deeper and deeper with the rest
of the stuff.

So I get past all that, and out of nowhere, My mother calls and say that she is going to kill herself for real this time. Mom tells me I have nothing to live for and, none of her kids are with her, they where taken away, She can't get the other ones in D.C, and then mom ask me to come to New Jersey. Somewhere in the back of my mind I think I can help my mother this time. So I go to my foster mom Vera and I ask her if she would keep my son for a week, while I go down to New Jersey to check on my mother. Vera tells me that she will. At this point I have godparents who Vera introduced me to. They accept me like I was with child and all the baggage that I came with. My godparents tell me don't go. They don't think it's safe. They continue to say it's no telling what your mother will do when you go down their Angie. I'm like hey, this is my mother and if I can help her I will.

Healing words

Don't put your self in harms way, take time to think before you act on something.

Chapter 8: Growing up

I leave my apartment and I leave my son, I figure that I will be back in a week. I get to New Jersey . My mom doesn't really have a place to stay. She's in motel to motel. Mom is telling me how she feels depressed and that she's not going to make it so I just try and console mom and be there for her. We get a room then the next day comes mom says I'm going out to do my little work and make sure we have stuff. So mom goes out and works at night then comes in and say lets go to the casino. We go to the casino and mom spends every dollar were we don't have any food. We don't know where we are going to sleep. Mom spent all the money for the hotel, for food to eat and I'm hungry. Now I'm thinking what are we suppose to do? Mom steals somebody money by pick pocketing them. Now we have the money to get a hotel so we check in. Mom also gets food for us to eat and we talk for awhile. I get the phone and call to talk to my son. It seems like Otis is getting bigger and bigger because he is talking like a big kid. A week and a half passes and I'm still in New Jersey with mom, waiting for mom to give me the money to go back home. I'm ready to go back home. I've been away from my son for to long and really I'm not trying to stay out here too much longer. Mom tells me that she needs me a little while longer so I say okay I'll stay a few more days but I want to get back home to my son. It's been close to two weeks, and still I can't go back home because there's no money to send me back home.

Mom gets this guy she had met and of course he's a pimp. She chooses him as her pimp. After choosing him he starts paying for the hotel bill he's making sure we have food to eat and anything else we need. Mom leaves and goes to work and she does not come back. Mom is gone for awhile. Now the hotel fees are due and its check out time. The hotel clerk asks if I have the money for the room and I don't. The only thing I have is the pimp's phone number. I call him and tell him my mom is not back yet and I ask him has he heard from her, he says no. Mom hasn't even checked in with him. I say the hotel is putting me out on the streets. Later on, I'm sitting out on the streets. The pimp comes and even though I don't know him, I get in the car. At this point anything is possible. He takes me to his apartment where he has two other working girls and he also has his kids living there. He says to me I don't understand why your mother is doing this. I respect you but what I don't respect about your mother is that she would leave her eighteen-year-old child with nothing and then expect a pimp to protect her child like she would. He says to me you know the game but you have never been out prostituting. I wouldn't even do that to you. If you stay here and watch the kids for me while the girls are out working that's all I expect from you Angie. Until I can find your mom and when I find her then you can go back with her.

I end up staying there a couple of days. I'm contacting my son and talking to my foster mom Vera and godparents. My godparents are worried and tell me they don't have the money to send me back home but they are trying to get it together. I want to see my son and I don't want to be here. A couple of day's passed and my mother finally calls. She talks to the pimp and asks where my daughter. She cries I want my daughter. She says that she was locked up. She's just crying and crying. The pimp tells mom I don't want your daughter you left her. I didn't put her out there on the streets like you expected me to do. He told her that's really cold that you would leave her in that type of environment, but I will put her in a cab and I will pay for the cab fare. Just tell me where to send her and the pimp does all of that so I meet up with my mother. Now I'm angry. I feel like mom put me in a situation where she wanted me to be out on the streets prostituting like she did.

I kept saying to myself why would my mother want that for her child? Why won't she let me have an opportunity to live my own life? Why would I follow in your footsteps as a prostitute? I don't say anything to mom I'm just bowling over. So we finally get to the room. Mom goes into the bathroom. I get on the phone crying and boohooing to my foster mom Vera. I'm telling her I'm ready to come home knowing that I'm probably going to loose my apartment. It's going on three weeks since I left to come to New Jersey I'm ready to go home; I miss my son like crazy. But I don't have any money I left my job, son and my apartment, what was I thinking, I can't help my mother. My foster mom Vera said she would call me back after she sees what my godparents can do. They are so worried now they say that my mother will try to have me out there prostituting, so they call back and say they will try and get as much money to send me back to Sacramento, California. I hang up the phone and walk in the bathroom and my mother has a pipe in her mouth; a crack pipe. I have never seen her smoke crack. Now I'm over the top. My mom is on crack . All of these diseases, so many things are running through my mind. Not only is mom a prostitute selling her body now she's an addict on top of all this. I came down here to help her because she said she was going to kill herself and all mom wanted to do was put me out on the street like her, or to help her make money to pay for her habit. I got a hold of myself after crying. I called my godmother and I told her I don't want to be here; my mom is hitting the pipe. I want to get home to my son and in that instant my godparents got out their credit card and called the airlines. I had my first class ticket back to California. In all that my mom is going off cursing and saying how could you leave me out here like this I'm your mother; I said I was going to send you back. Mom is still going off saying that you called the people on me. I didn't pay mother any attention; I waited until my godparents sent the money western union so I could catch a cab to the airport. They sent $100.00dollars. I took that cab down to the airport got on the next plan heading to Sacramento, CA so I could be with my son. Once back home I see my son.

He was so happy he ran into my arms mama, mama, I pee, pee on the pot. Grandma taught me how to pee, pee on the pot. He just talked and talked to me and told me everything that was happening to him. Otis tells me mommy I love you don't leave me no more. At that point I say I will never leave you again or ever again trust my mother. I will never again walk away from you son. You are most important to me. I will not put myself in a situation where my son feels like I have been away from him to long. Like they said in one of those movies "we ride together, we die together". That was my "motto", for my son and I. Wherever I went he went. From that point on I would be the best mother I could be to my son. I get back on my feet. I got another apartment and job. I was still young. I met a lot of men. I got myself into lots of situations I shouldn't have gotten myself into. I was very promiscuous. I tried not to get myself so far gone out there to the point where I would harm my son. I called my godparents' one day. We had to sit down and talk. We sat down and my godparents told me about Jesus. They were big on getting saved and being a Christian and living for God.
I said you know what I'll try it. So I got saved.

Healing words

Sometimes you can't help some one, so when you know you can't help them don't try you will only hurt your self.

Chapter 9: I'm feeling myself

It is the beginning of 1992. Living a Christian life was incredibly hard. I'm 19 years old and have felt all along that I needed someone in my life. So, I began praying for a Husband that's what my godparents told me to do because sex be for marriage is a sin. Unfortunately, I get no response from god. Instead of me staying on the prayerful track, I started hanging out in the Heights, Del Paso Heights. This is where all the action was. I was going to have me some fun now . I began at the "Touch of Class" no luck there. Then it was on to the Elks struck out there to. Then one day while walking on Grand Ave with my sister and friends this fine guy pulled over and asks me my name. I'm asking myself; "who does this guy thinks he is"? He looks like a gangster with all this long hair and pimped out clothes, but I tell him my name. He then introduced himself as John. He then asks for my phone number but I am not too sure about him. By this time, one of my homeboys named Gable pulls up and starts talking to John and I ask Gable if John is cool. He said they go way back and he's really cool. So I give John my number and that same day he calls me and ask me out. Of course I tell him yes and the next day we go out and have a good time together.

John is asking me about being in a relationship but I don't even know him and he want to be all serious. I just got back into the swing of things but he is so fine I just can't help it so we start seeing one another. We start a relationship and John moves in with me. All of this happened so fast that within the next couple of months I was pregnant. I tell John I'm pregnant and he asks me to marry him so I say yes because I didn't want to have another baby without being married. John and I were married and not long after our wedding, he was incarcerated. He is in jail and I'm pregnant. John and ask him what he did. He's trying to lie and say it's a misunderstanding so I call the jail and they say he was with an under age girl. I'm devastated but I really did not know him like I should have and now I'm married to him.

He gets two years in prison and now he wants be there to see our baby born. John had lots of secrets. I was not aware that he had been with some one when he was trying to get with me. The other girl was very upset to learn that I was pregnant. I did not find out all of this until he went to jail. Now it's 1993 and I have my baby and it's a girl and she is so beautiful and very healthy. I feel like John should be a part of her life so I decide to stick by him. The kids and I start going to see John in prison every weekend and he is telling me he's going to be a good father when he got out and he is sorry for what he has done. John says we will be a family soon. This was short lived. I get a call from him that they gave him some more time for assaulting an officer. Two additional years added on to his time. I'm ready to stop dealing with him so I stop going to see him and started clubbing again. John is forgotten. It's 1994 and I'm having some financial problems. I am rethinking my life over and asking myself what am I doing?

I begin to remember how my life was when I was serving God. I start to pray and I decided to give my life back to Jesus. I immediately felt much better. I called my god mother, Roberta and told her that I needed a church home. I also called my Aunt Jill and told her to. I started going to church with my aunt but it was not really spirit filled and I really struggled trying to seek out God. So my godmother gave me a call and told me that she has this church that she wanted me to visit. I told her that I did not want to go to a church with all old people. She tells me it not like that so I go. I end up loving it there I become a member and start to grow in my walk with God.

Then I get a call from Washington, DC about my sister and brother Charmain and Gregory. They were going to be adopted. I told the social worker that I would like to try and get them. We make arraignments for me to go to DC and get them. It 1996 and I go down to DC and get them and they come and live with me. They are having so many problems adapting I try to get them involved in sports and the youth programs at church. A year has passed Charmain is really out of control so she tells her teacher that I beat her and they come out and check all the kids and find no abuse and ask me can she stay and I tell them no. I will not put my kids in harms way and I still had to think about Gregory so the social work took Charmain. The worker calls all the time to see if I would take Charmain back but I don't.

So now the kids and I are doing well and John calls to ask me why am I seeking an annulment? I tell him that it is not working and I want to move on. He then asks me if I will come to see him. I go see him and he's saying he wants his family and he's been going to church and changing is life around and asks will I take him back. So I say yes during this time Gregory won't to go back to DC with chairman and I try to tell him that's not a good idea. But he starts stealing and getting in trouble at school so I let him go about a year later.

John gets out and come to live with us but he has to register as a sex offender. I'm praying everyday that I should not have taken him back. We lasted about five more months and John starts cheating on me. So I just finish my paper with the courts and get my annulment. John ends up going back to prison for rape. I don't know who it was but I was glad I left him alone. It's going to be hard to tell my daughter about her dad. However, when the time comes, I will and let her now she was created in love.

Healing Words

Don't let your flesh over take you. Your mind is strong Even if your body is not.

Chapter 10: Friendship-part 1

It 1999 I meet this young lady in church name Savona she about two years younger. We sing me, and Savona is in the choir together. we start hanging out, and it funny because I had just prayed and ask god to send me some young friends because all I had was older people in my life and thou that was good, I had found a church that had young people that loved Jesus just as much as I did so Savona and I became very close friends we did everything together. We went on diets together went to all the church functions together. I felt so good about this. I had finally had a friend I could trust that was a female.

One day this guy name Lee came to the church and he was so cute and I liked him and he was singing in the choir to. So I told Savona that I liked Lee and she told me she liked Demon. So we would talk about them from time to time. We thought maybe they could be the men we were praying for. Savona told me that Lee works with the youth and I know that she did too. What was I thinking? Savona come and tells me some good things about Lee. We start to have some good conversations but it looks like Savona is doing too much talking to Lee. Savona is calling him on the phone. She tells me Lee asks if we wanted to go to the other church functions with him. We go but I'm feeling funny but I don't say anything. After the function she starts to ask Lee about some girl he was talking to, this was enough for me. The next day I ask her do you like Lee. She says no! I said it looks like it. I will not be mad. I just want you to tell me the truth about how you feel about him. I told her that our friendship meant more to me then a man but she still says no. Come to find out they have been going out all over the town all in the bay area on carriage rides .Now I'm devastated. This is my friend and she lied to me and I have to see her and him smiling in my face singing together. Now I am wondering if I should leave the church. I'm hurt and I feel rejected by someone close to me again. I know running will not solve my problems and the devil wants to tear me from my church. I start praying and asking God to fix me and help me not to be bitter because Savona and Lee did what they did. I thought that Lee was the one. After thinking about it I realized he could not be the one for me, what's mine no man can take from me.

I prayed to the Lord let them be happy together. I'm not saying it was easy but it was not healthy for me to stay angry. It took about one year to get over this. One night the Lord told me to go to her. I finally went to Savona and told her that I forgive her and wish her the best. But she was not doing too well. Lee had stopped wanting to see her. He was telling people that he did not want her coming over his new house. They had a big blow up at church. Some people would be happy but I was not. I told her that God sent me over here to let you know that I love you and Jesus loves you. I thought it would be hard to go through that and come out and be ok. When I left Savona's house I just thanked God that he saved me from that kind of headache.

Chapter 10: Friendship-part 2

In 2001, God then blessed me with a new friend name Marie she was married to Virginia my old foster mother grandson. We knew one another but never really talked. Marie was having some problems with her husband so our friendship started by me ministering to her telling her about Jesus. She knew him but didn't have a personal relationship with him so we talked a lot about Jesus. I never told her what to do about her marital problems. I just listened. He was very mean to her. He would stay out all night I told her I can't tell you what to do you have to go to God if you want your marriage. I also told her that she must wait for a change if she really wanted her marriage. I prayed with her but it hurt me to see her heart saddened. No one should have to go through this but I never told her that and I started telling my self I would never go through this.

Marie helped me to love myself. She did not care what was going on in her life. She kept her head up and told me don't worry about what people say about you. She had this down and this is what I needed. We were like sisters. We were inseparable. This was my girl. We raised our kids together took them every where. We went Red Lobster every weekend. We would take the kids to San Francisco and six-flags just having fun.

During this time I meet Alisha. I was really scared to get close to any one but she needed a friend. Alisha's father was a preacher but she really was looking for something and just needed a friend. God stepped in and we became very good friends. I have been there for her and she has been there for me. We meet at Wells Fargo. Marie would watch my kids when I went to work so I thought it would be god for them to get to know one another but Marie didn't try to go there so I made time for both of them. Marie would get kind of huffy when I said I was out with Alisha I think because Marie needed to keep the connection. Alisha Marie and I would talk about me wanting to get married all the time.

I finally met some one in 2003 named Mark. My friends seemed very happy for me. When I started hanging out with Mark. Marie wanted to be right in the middle but I didn't want that and I thought she would understand that. After what had already happened to me I did not want to have a replay of my previous incident. She started staying away more and I put my all in to my relationship. Marie and I still talked but it just was not the same. One day the kids got in to it and Marie told me she was threw dealing with me. This was so hard for me because no matter what we would always come back and start right were we left off but not this time. I was there when she had her second child, I had seen him growing up and she wanted to see my baby girl Christina grows up. We would see one another at church. Yes, we go to the same church and barely spoke to one another. At this time I realized that God placed all these people in my life for me to help them and for them to help me with a lot of trust problems. I realize that I lost my friend and I really miss her.

Life had to move on so started taking Alisha to church with me and her spirits were looking up. But in 2005 Alisha lost her sister in a fatal shooting. I tried to be there for her and her family. She had to take on the responsibility of taking care of her sister kids. Me being married it was hard for us to hang out as much but we still hang out when we have the time and are still very good friends. And God has given me a few more good people in my life all ages so he did answer my prayers in his time.

Healing Words

Needing to be accepted some time will cause rejection, be a friend to your self first learn to love your self, because then you can determine who's good for your life.

Chapter 11: My Will Not God's Will

It now 2003 and I have just open my hair salon and I also meet Mark thing are looking good for me. Mark was my neighbor and I thought he looked like a hard working man. We met one another at a Grant football game. Prior to us meeting we used to wave at one another and I would hunk my horn almost every day when I saw him. When we finally met I said I'm the girl in the little brown car that you wave too. I told him my name is Angie and I gave him my business card and told him to call me sometime. He did the next day and we just hit it off. We talked for about two weeks over the phone. He told me he went to his uncle's church and he worked construction. He was kind of quite but that was ok. I ended up sending him a rose and a card. I had some people that owned a flower shop so I had them deliver it to him. Maybe I was to forward but I just wanted him to know that I thought he was a nice guy and I thought that if you treat some one like you would want to be treated it would come back to you.

I told Mark I was looking for a husband and he told me he had been praying for a wife so I thought this was a good fit. It had been 6 years since I have been with a man sexually. See I was waiting for God to bless me so mark and I are talking about marriage we would take long walks just laughing and talking. Mark was so nice to me and my kids.

I remember a time I got sick and mark came over and brought me some soup and cooked diner for my kids he would do things like this all the time like help the kids with there homework he was such a good guy. I got frighten and felt like if I wait to long I might lose him so we sleep together Now I feel so bad. I feel that I let God down so I repent. But that's just not good enough. We rushed and got married within three months of knowing one another. See I think I knew God a little better than Mark so I was trying to fix my sins. This is impossible. What you do in the dark will come to the light. Mark and I had no counseling. We ran to Reno and got married. I didn't even tell my pastor whom I had been under for 10 years that I got married.

The marriage started off with so many financial hardships because I had just opened my beauty salon and I had bills which I did not let my new husband

Mark know about. My husband Mark ended up paying them shortly after we where married. After he paid the bills then Marks car broke down and he lost his job from a work injury. We tried to stay positive and do a lot of family activities but Mark was way younger then me and was folding under the prissier of being married and paying bills so Mark's attitude changed for the worst.

Mark then stopped wanting to go to church. He started having a problem with my son and my son's dad. I end up sending my son to his dads because we argued every day about little things my son Otis would do. Mark was jealous of the relationship my son's and I had. I put one and two together and realized that Mark was also jealous of my son's father. I thought with my son gone it would get better. He was ok with my daughter because her father was in jail but it just got worse. For every good day there was two bad days. I'm not feeling good. I'm sick all the time so I go to the doctor and find out I'm pregnant. But he keeps me stressed so much he doesn't want me to run my salon because there's a barbershop next door to me. He's mad about everything.

I end up losing my baby. I was three months pregnant. When I get home from the hospital he goes off and say I killed is baby. I wanted to say no you did but I stay quite. All I wanted was some rest. But he would not stop going off so I call a friend and ask her to pick me up and I stay over there for the night. The next day I go home and he's all better but I know now I'm in a verbally abusive relationship. We were about a year into this marriage and we move from my house and try a new change. I am thinking that maybe it will be better but it's the same so I tell Mark he has to go. So he goes back to his uncles and auntie house. He is gone for about one week and I find out I'm a month pregnant so he comes back home. Mark says I'm going to treat you better now that we're having a baby and I don't want you to lose this baby. Mark does not have any kids so he's happy at first but that does not last long.

Mark starts fussing again scaring me like he's going to hit me. I'm working trying to run my salon but he saying that I'm sleeping with the guy at the barbershop and maybe it's not his baby. I'm three months now and this is all I can take. Easter comes and my stepbrothers on my dads side Robby and Royce and my son are all over. The night before Easter one of the kids must have bumped up against the stove because the gas was turned on and my brothers had walked to the store and my son and daughter were at home watching TV. Mark goes off and says that some one is trying to kill him. Now mine you I'm upstairs sleeping so we would all have died. My kids and I are the only one gone. My brothers walked up a few minutes later and Mark is cussing saying he will kill someone trying to kill him. My stepbrothers are white so they don't know what to do and they are only 14 years old. My son is tripping he's 16 years old and my daughter is used to this so she is looking at him crazy. Then Mark goes and calls the police on the kids and they come out and believe this dummy and Mark really wants to put this on my son. But that's not going to happen. My son doesn't want to kill me. So the police start questioning my son like he did it, telling him he can be charged as an adult and I tell the police to get out my house! My son did not try to kill anyone. I tell my son to go upstairs and don't say anything else. The next day I put my stepbrothers on the train back to Fresno and I tell Mark that he has to leave. He comes to him self like he is a schizophrenic and says he is sorry and he knows he has to go.

Mark goes back home to Arkansas He stays for about three months and says he want to come home. I'm seven months pregnant and missing him and want him to be there when I have the baby. So I let him come back and now I'm thinking I 'm acting just like my mom. I am telling myself that this can't be how love is to be. But I feel like I did this by having sex before we were married so just deal with it. I really believe that I love him. I now realize that I am a victim of battered woman's syndrome. So Mark is here and it's ok for a little time. He's not as verbally abusive. The time has come for me to have the baby, however, I'm having some medical problems. The baby is not having a lot of movement so the doctor tells me I need to have a C-section. I'm very scared that something is wrong with my baby girl. But she comes out fine very healthy. She is very fair skin with straight hair so now that's a problem with Mark. Because we're not light skinned and his mom is high yellow. I think he forgot that my mother is not black. Now he saying the baby may not be his and he says the baby looks like my son. For the first two weeks the baby was big Otis's baby. Now I'm stitched up can't really move and I'm in pain. I am emotionally tired and this is all he can do to hurt me. This is supposed to be a positive time but it's not. We eventually get over this.

Mark goes back to work and it seems to be going ok but I'm not up cooking every day. The house is not spotless and Mark's job does not pay that good so I'm paying most of the bills from the money I got from selling the salon. Yes I sold it trying to be a good wife and mother. Mark said the baby was not going to go to work with me to the ghetto in Del Paso Heights. My son's aunt bought it from me but things are no better. He's still yelling because the baby's crying and I'm not doing what I'm told. I'm being called bitches, tramps and Mark threatens to hit me with chairs. So I tell Mark you can stay but I got to go. This is not what I want. I don't want my girls to see this. Areionna is getting older and this is not a good relationship so Mark goes back to Arkansas.

Now he's calling and telling me he want to come home . I prayed and asked God to help me and he did but Mark just would not except that it was over and just keep calling. I told Mark please stop calling I am trying to put the pieces to my life back together. Mark just would not take me serious and just would not leave me a loan. I finally told Mark I have got my foster license and could not be in a domestic violence relationship. Mark said that he had changed and would come home and help, with the kids. I told mark that's not how it works but he did not care he just keep trying to come home. For the next three month Mark just keep calling telling me that he got a good job and stopped smoking weed and knows what it take to be a family man he really sounded sincere. Mark had started to ware me down. I wanted to believe that he changed this time so I broke down and told Mark that I would come to Arkansas to visit and if he had really changed I would discuses him coming home. I felt that if Mark had changed he would be able to visit with us and talk about are future and what needed to be dune to make the marriage work. That following week I maid arrangements for my foster kid to go in to placement that next month for to weeks because foster kids could not go out of state which I guess I could understand and I was not quit sure how Mark would act. I went on a booked are plane ticket to Arkansas. Later that week I had received a call from my foster care agency that my kids were go home to their mother so it looked like everything was working out for me. I went on to Arkansas that following week. It Sunday and we get their and Mark is at the Air port waiting for us we see Mark and he looks like he just won a million dollars. I go over and give him a big kiss and huge and he so happy he give Areionna and Christine a huge and kiss and said that he missed us. Mark went said that Christina has gotten so big and pretty and looked just like hem but the truth was she looked just like me.

Later that evening we get settled in and everything thing is going so well mark seems to be so happy. The next day we go and see all of Marks family members and every one was so happy to see Christina Marks father MR H come by the house to see his grand daughter and just fell in love with her he asked me did she need any thing I said no but he still felt that he had to get her something so MR H went out and bough her a walker I thought that was so nice. Later on that even MR H ask me what I wonted to do about my living arrangements I responded that I live in California and was doing well he then said that you cant live their and your husband lives in Arkansas so if you move heir I will by you and Mark a house and you both can work on your relationship I thought this was the best thing that could happing to us but for some reason Mark did not later that night mark was acting rely funny I just ignored him and keep on having a god time the next day we went sight seeing and it was so beautiful in Arkansas I thought to my self that this place would be just the right place to raise my kids and we would have are new house. I then asked him why did that even matter we got to have are own home. Mark just stopped talking and I went to bed.

The next day I asked to use his car to go to the store, Mark lost it start tripping. He was saying that I didn't like to have sex with him. I did not know were all this was coming from I even tried to talk to him but he proceeded with cussing me out and telling me he was not going to kiss my ass. I then told him that good just take me to a hotel and tomorrow I can go home. Mark told me that I could go but I could not take my baby I just had to laugh I went on and started to pack my stuff. Mark was laughing and acting like I was not serious. I put my stuff out side and told him lets go. Mark then slammed my stuff in the trunk and we drove and drove. I asked Mark were are we going you pasted nine hotels. Mark did not say a word, about thirty minute passed Mark pulls up it to a woodsy area I didn't no what to do. Mark then told me to get out because he was tired of my shit. So I did and I just started to pray Mark was acting liked he was going to run me over the girls were crying and so scared . At this time a car was pulling up so Mark stop the car and told me to get in so I did he then drove to some more woods were their were no cars. He told me to get out again and this time take your daughter Areionna with you. I told him you will have to kill me out here if you think that I am going to be stuck in the wood with my daughter you are going to have to take her with You. He kept yelling take your daughter and keep saying you will have to kill me this went on for about twenty minutes. Then Mark through my stuff out the car and pushed me down and asked me why do I make him do this. All I could think is this man is crazy and if I get out of this he will never see me again. I just started to cry Mark finally told me to get in the car and he would take me to a hotel. We got to the hotel and Mark put my stuff out and told me I could not have my daughter Christina. I lost it I started to scream and ran in to the hotel and called his dad his dad told me to call the police so we did about five minute after the police got their Mark pulled up and said that he was just trying to spend time with his daughter the police told him to leave and don't come back over here, they also told me to get a restraining order on him when I get home and a Divorce. Mark left and start to call me he even sent his aunts to come and check up on me they were trying to get me to stay but I had already called the airlines and changed my ticket to leave out the next day. Mark called and said that he would take us to the airport and would not bother us. So I let him it was a very long ride we never said a word to each other.

I got home and tried to put my life back together about two weeks later Mark started to call and tell me that he was sorry and he did not mean to be so out of control. He went on to say that he was homeless he lost his job and he had to move out, and his family would not let him stay with them. I stared to fill sorry for him and the calls were coming every day he just wore me down . A month after the calls I sent him a bus ticket I could not leave my husband homeless. Mark got home and promised to go to work and be a good husband and father. For about three weeks it was good he got a job and went to church a few times.

During this time my son moved back and Mark started to go back to is old was smoking weed and drinking he started asking me for my money and I would not give it to him. Mark was only paying half of the rent he did not help with the kids he did not even help with is own child I was paying all the other bills and the kids so I felt that my money was mine . It just started to get bad Mark had said he was going to bust my teeth out of my mouth. My son was their and said that he was not going to bust my teeth out so Mark got in to my son face and asked him did he want some of him and my son did not but he was not going to let him hit me. Mark then started after me saying that I let my son disrespect him and he will hurt every one in this house, me and kids ran straight to the neighbors she had heard it all so she called the police and I got in my car and met them at Rite-Aid the police came and told me that because he did not hit me they could not do anything and they knew his boss and they would call him. Mark's boss was their boss at one time he had retired from the sheriff department this was unbelievable. I went home and told Mark that he had to leave. I would give him two weeks to find him some were to live. Mark left after the two weeks and I filled for divorce and left Mark.

Mark gave me such a hard time with custody I had to fight like my life deepened on it. In the end I got custody Mark end up having another kid and moved back to Arkansas he left heir baby and Christina . I am just glad he's out of my life. I am over the pain and I have forgiven him and my self and I can talk to him and be ok I don't ever want to be with him. I have peace in my life it took years but I am good and putting my life back to gather. I am working at a shop doing hair, I have also starting my new book " Should I Go Or Should I Stay " My son Otis has graduated for high school and is in college and working at a local shoe store. Areionna is in the tenth grad now with a 3.0 GPA she's is good in school but don't get me wrong she is giving me a run for my money being a teen. Christina is in preschool she think she's a stare and grown were working with her she no wear near four more like thirty three. The rest of my family Crystal, Tamika, Chairman, PePe. Aaron, Carlos. Gregory they are all tiring to make it. Some are in jail and some have police records but their trying to make it with the hand they were dealt . Mother is out off prison and still working her old position some times things don't change I have forgiven her and do talk to her from time, and help her when I can but were not close. Put I keep praying God is able. Know that life can be challenging but god has a plan and when your going threw it's just god's way of strengthening you so don't give up there is grate reward at the end. Remember not to focus on the path but keep reaching for the goal.

Healing Words

I realize that I am a queen and a descendant of the most high I deserve the best.
Put god first and he will bring it to past what ever it may be.

Acknowledgment:

I would like to thank those who have made a positive impact on my life; my pastor Parnell M Lovelace Jr. and are first lady Diana. Linda Williams and Patricia Gordon who helped me in editing my book. I would also like to thank my family and friends

Special Thanks'

Jesus for being my heavenly father.
Pastor Parnell for being my spiritual father.
Mr. Coob for creating the cover of the book, you did a wonderful job.